WELCOME TO Hawaii!

LEARN ABOUT THE HISTORY OF...

The Polynesians • The Big Island • Hilo • Kailua-Kona •
Waimea • Maui • Kahului • Lahaina • Wailea • Oahu •
Honolulu • Waikiki • Kailua • Kauai • Lihue • Hanalei •
Poipu • Modern History • Historical Hawaiians • King
Kamehameha I • Queen Liliuokalani • Duke Kahanamoku •
Mary Kawena Pukui • Pearl Harbor • Iolani Palace •
Puuhonua o Honaunau & Kalaupapa National Historical
Parks • Traditional Hawaiian Sports • Surfing • Canoeing •
Hula • Makahiki Games • Hawaiian Boxing • Hawaiian
Foods • Poi • Kalua Pig • Poke •

ILLUSTRATED WITH HISTORICAL PHOTOS

INTRODUCTION

The Hawaiian Islands are a chain of eight major islands located in the Pacific Ocean, specifically in the North Pacific region. They are a part of the United States and are situated in the state of Hawaii. The islands are known for their unique geography, tropical climate, and diverse wildlife, making them one of the most popular tourist destinations in the world.

The eight major Hawaiian Islands are Hawaii, Maui, Oahu, Kauai, Molokai, Lanai, Niihau, and Kahoolawe. These islands are the result of volcanic activity that occurred over millions of years, with some of the islands still being formed today. Each island has its own distinct characteristics, ranging from the active volcanoes on Hawaii Island to the stunning beaches of Maui and the bustling city life on Oahu.

The Hawaiian Islands are known for their beautiful landscapes, which include beaches, mountains, waterfalls, and lush forests. Visitors can explore the islands by hiking, snorkeling, surfing, or simply lounging on the beach. The islands are also home to a rich cultural history, with Hawaiian traditions and customs still being celebrated and practiced today.

The Hawaiian Islands are also known for their unique wildlife. The islands are home to a number of endangered species, including the Hawaiian monk seal, the Hawaiian hoary bat, and the Hawaiian honeycreeper bird. Visitors can learn more about these species by visiting the various wildlife sanctuaries and conservation areas located on the islands.

In addition to their natural beauty, the Hawaiian Islands also have a rich cultural history. The islands were first settled by Polynesians more than a thousand years ago and have a unique and rich culture that is still celebrated and practiced today. Visitors can experience this culture by attending traditional Hawaiian ceremonies, watching hula dancing, or trying traditional Hawaiian food.

The Hawaiian Islands are a unique and beautiful part of the world that offer visitors a diverse range of experiences, from outdoor activities to cultural experiences. Whether you're looking to relax on the beach, explore the mountains, or learn about Hawaiian history and culture, the Hawaiian Islands have something to offer everyone.

THE POLYNESIANS

The history of Polynesians in Hawaii is a complex and fascinating story that spans over a thousand years. The Polynesians were the first people to settle in Hawaii and their culture and traditions have had a profound impact on the islands to this day.

The Polynesians are believed to have originated from Southeast Asia and made their way across the Pacific by canoe. They settled in various parts of the Pacific, including the islands of Samoa, Tonga, and Fiji, before eventually making their way to Hawaii around the 5th century AD.

The first Polynesian settlers in Hawaii were likely from the Marquesas Islands, which are located about 1,200 miles to the northeast of Hawaii. These early settlers brought with them a rich culture and a strong connection to the sea. They were skilled navigators and fishermen, and they relied heavily on the ocean for their survival.

Over time, the Polynesians who settled in Hawaii developed their own unique culture, which was influenced by their interactions with other Polynesian groups and by the resources available on the islands. They built complex societies, with chiefs and commoners, and developed a complex system of agriculture and land use.

One of the most significant cultural developments of the Polynesians in Hawaii was the creation of the ahupua'a system. This system divided the land into pie-shaped sections, each of which included a portion of the shoreline and extended up into the mountains. The ahupua'a system ensured that each community had access to the resources they needed to survive, including fish from the ocean and crops from the land.

The Polynesians in Hawaii also developed a complex system of religion and spirituality. They worshipped a pantheon of gods and goddesses, and their religious practices were closely tied to the natural world. They believed that the gods and goddesses controlled the weather, the ocean, and the land, and they offered sacrifices and prayers to ensure a bountiful harvest and good fortune.

In the late 18th century, the arrival of European explorers and traders began to change the face of Hawaii. The Polynesians were introduced to new technologies and goods, including firearms and alcohol, which had a profound impact on their culture. The arrival of Europeans also brought diseases to the islands, which had a devastating effect on the Polynesian population.

In 1819, King Kamehameha II abolished the traditional Polynesian religious practices and replaced them with Christianity. This marked a significant turning point in the history of the Polynesians in Hawaii and had a profound impact on their culture and way of life.

Despite these changes, the Polynesians in Hawaii continued to maintain their connection to their ancestral roots. They passed down their traditions and cultural practices from generation to generation, and their language and customs continue to be an important part of the Hawaiian identity.

The Polynesians in Hawaii are a vibrant and diverse community, with a rich culture and a strong connection to the land and the sea. They continue to celebrate their heritage through music, dance, and traditional practices, and they play a vital role in the cultural and economic life of the islands. The Polynesians in Hawaii are a testament to the resilience and adaptability of human cultures, and their story is an important part of the history of Hawaii and the Pacific.

HiSTORY OF THE Hawaiian ISLANDS:

Hawaii

The island of Hawaii, also known as the Big Island, is the largest of the eight main islands in the Hawaiian Island chain. It has a rich and diverse history that spans thousands of years, beginning with the arrival of Polynesian voyagers and continuing through modern times.

In the late 18th century, British explorer Captain James Cook arrived in Hawaii and established contact with the native Hawaiian people. Cook's arrival marked the beginning of significant changes to Hawaiian society and culture, as European and American traders and missionaries began arriving in greater numbers.

By the early 19th century, the Hawaiian Islands had become an important stopover point for traders and sailors, and the kingdom of Hawaii was established with King Kamehameha I as its first ruler. During this time, the islands also became a popular destination for missionaries, who brought with them their own religion and culture.

In the late 19th century, Hawaii became an important center for the sugar industry, with wealthy plantation owners dominating the economy and politics of the islands. This led to a period of significant social and economic change, as Hawaiian workers were brought in to work on the plantations, and the native Hawaiian population was pushed into poverty and disenfranchisement.

In 1959, Hawaii became the 50th state in the United States, and the Big Island has since become a popular destination for tourists from around the world. Today, the island is known for its beautiful natural landscapes, rich cultural heritage, and unique blend of Hawaiian and American culture. Visitors to the island can explore its stunning beaches, hike its towering volcanoes, and experience the unique Hawaiian way of life.

Maui

Maui is the second-largest island in the Hawaiian Island chain and has a rich history that dates back thousands of years. The island was first settled by Polynesians who arrived in the area around 600 AD. These early settlers established small communities throughout the island and developed a unique culture and way of life.

The island of Maui was ruled by various chiefs or Ali'i who were responsible for maintaining the island's social and political order. One of the most famous chiefs was Kamehameha, who unified the Hawaiian Islands and established the Kingdom of Hawaii in the late 18th century.

During the 19th century, Maui became a hub for the sugar industry, with large plantations being established throughout the island. The island's economy boomed, and many immigrants from China, Japan, and the Philippines were brought in to work on the plantations. However, this also led to social tensions and labor disputes, which culminated in the famous strike of 1904, where 10,000 sugar workers went on strike.

Maui played an important role in World War II as well. The island was home to several military bases, and the town of Lahaina was used as a rest and relaxation spot for soldiers. Maui was also the site of the Battle of Niihau, where a Japanese pilot crash-landed on the island and was captured by local residents.

Maui is known for its stunning natural beauty, diverse wildlife, and popular tourist attractions. The island is home to some of the best beaches in the world, including Kaanapali Beach and Wailea Beach. Maui is also famous for its scenic Road to Hana, which winds through lush rainforests and stunning waterfalls.

The history of Maui is a rich and complex one that has been shaped by the island's unique geography, culture, and people. From the early Polynesian settlers to the sugar plantation era and the events of World War II, Maui has played an important role in the history of Hawaii and continues to be a popular destination for visitors from around the world.

Oahu

The island of Oahu, also known as "The Gathering Place," is the third-largest of the Hawaiian Islands and is home to over 70% of the state's population. Its history is a rich tapestry of ancient Polynesian culture, European exploration, and modern American influence.

Polynesians first settled on Oahu around 1,000 years ago, traveling from the Marquesas Islands and Tahiti in search of new land. They brought with them their unique culture, including their language, religion, and way of life. The ancient Hawaiians developed a complex social system, with chiefs and commoners, and a deep reverence for the land and sea.

In the late 18th century, the first European explorers arrived on Oahu. The British explorer Captain James Cook was the first European to make contact with the island in 1778. He named the archipelago the "Sandwich Islands" in honor of his patron, the Earl of Sandwich. Cook's arrival marked the beginning of a period of immense change for Hawaii, as Europeans began to introduce new technologies, plants, and animals to the islands.

In 1795, the chief of Oahu, Kamehameha I, began a campaign to unify the Hawaiian Islands under his rule. He eventually succeeded in 1810, creating the Kingdom of Hawaii. During the 19th century, the kingdom thrived under the rule of

Kamehameha's descendants, who welcomed foreign visitors and developed a booming sugar industry.

In 1893, however, a group of American businessmen and politicians overthrew the Hawaiian monarchy and established a provisional government. The following year, the Republic of Hawaii was formed, and in 1898, the United States annexed Hawaii as a territory. Oahu became an important military base for the US during World War II, as the Japanese bombed Pearl Harbor on December 7, 1941, leading to the United States' entry into the war.

Oahu is a vibrant and diverse island, home to a rich blend of cultures and traditions. Its capital city, Honolulu, is a bustling metropolis with a thriving tourism industry, while the island's North Shore is a world-famous surf spot. Oahu is also home to several military installations, including the Joint Base Pearl Harbor-Hickam and the Marine Corps Base Hawaii.

Kauai

Kauai is one of the oldest and most beautiful islands in Hawaii. The island has a rich history that dates back over a thousand years. The first settlers to arrive on Kauai were Polynesians from the Marquesas Islands around 500 AD. They brought with them their culture, language, and way of life, which helped shape the island's unique identity.

The early Polynesians who settled on Kauai were skilled farmers and fishermen. They lived in small communities along the coast and in the valleys, where they cultivated taro, sweet potato, and other crops. They also fished in the abundant waters around the island, using canoes and nets made from local materials.

Over time, Kauai's population grew, and the island became home to a powerful chiefdom. The island was divided into several districts, each ruled by a local chief or ali'i. The most famous of these chiefs was Kaumuali'i, who ruled Kauai in the late 18th and early 19th centuries. He was known for his intelligence, diplomacy, and skill as a warrior.

In the late 1700s, Kauai came into contact with European explorers and traders. The first Europeans to arrive on Kauai were the Spanish, who visited the island in 1778. They were followed by British and American traders, who established a thriving trade in sandalwood, which was highly prized in China. In 1810, Kauai was united with the other Hawaiian islands under the rule of King Kamehameha I. However, the island remained largely autonomous, and its chiefs continued to wield considerable power.

During the mid-19th century, Kauai underwent a period of rapid change. The sugar industry was introduced, and vast plantations were established across the island. Immigrants from China, Japan, Portugal, and the Philippines were brought in to work on the plantations, and Kauai's population became more diverse.

In the 20th century, Kauai continued to evolve,

becoming a popular destination for tourists. The island's stunning natural beauty, including its pristine beaches, lush rainforests, and majestic mountains, drew visitors from around the world.

Kauai is a thriving community with a rich cultural heritage. The island's residents continue to celebrate their traditions and way of life, while embracing new ideas and technologies. Kauai's history is a testament to the resilience and ingenuity of the people who have called this beautiful island home for centuries.

Molokai

Molokai is one of the Hawaiian Islands, located in the central Pacific Ocean. The island has a rich history, which dates back to ancient times when Polynesians first settled there. The island has gone through a lot of changes since then, and its history is marked by several significant events and influences.

According to legend, Molokai was discovered by a chief named Kamapua'a, who sailed to the island from Maui. The island was later populated by Polynesian settlers who arrived in large canoes from the Marquesas Islands. They brought with them a rich culture and traditions, which helped shape the island's identity and way of life.

The island's first major historical event occurred in the late 18th century when European explorers began arriving in the Hawaiian Islands. The first European to set foot on Molokai was Captain James Cook, who visited the island in 1778. Cook's arrival marked the beginning of a new era in Molokai's history, as the island became part of the global trade network and saw increased contact with outsiders.

In the early 19th century, Molokai was ruled by the powerful chief Kahekili, who was known for his military prowess and political savvy. Under his leadership, Molokai became a center of Hawaiian power and culture, and its people prospered. However, this period of peace and stability came to an end with the arrival of Christian missionaries, who sought to convert the island's inhabitants to their religion.

The introduction of Christianity to Molokai was followed by a wave of changes, including the imposition of new laws and customs, which had a profound impact on the island's culture and way of life. One of the most significant events in Molokai's history during this time was the construction of the Kalaupapa Leper Colony, which was established in 1866 to isolate people with leprosy from the rest of society. The colony became a symbol of the island's struggle to maintain its traditions and identity in the face of outside influences.

Molokai is a popular tourist destination, known for its stunning natural beauty and rich cultural heritage. The island's history is a testament to the resilience and strength of its people, who have

managed to overcome numerous challenges over the centuries to preserve their unique way of life. From the early Polynesian settlers to the present-day residents, Molokai's people continue to celebrate their heritage and remain committed to preserving the island's cultural and natural resources for future generations.

Lanai

The Hawaiian island of Lanai, also known as the Pineapple Island, has a rich and interesting history that dates back thousands of years. The island was first settled by Polynesians around 1,500 years ago, who lived off the land and sea by farming taro, fishing, and hunting wild game.

In the late 18th century, European explorers began visiting the Hawaiian islands, and in 1793, the British explorer Captain George Vancouver visited Lanai and named it after his friend, the navigator James Cook. During the early 19th century, the island was ruled by the powerful Maui chief, Kahekili II, who used Lanai as a strategic outpost to expand his territory. After Kahekili's death, the island was ruled by various chiefs until the 1850s, when the island was annexed by the Kingdom of Hawaii.

During the late 1800s, the island's history took a dramatic turn when James Dole, a young entrepreneur from Massachusetts, arrived on the island and established the Hawaiian Pineapple Company. Under Dole's leadership, the company transformed Lanai into the world's leading pineapple producer, bringing in thousands of workers from around the world to work in the fields and canneries.

The island remained under Dole's control until 1961, when he sold it to Castle & Cooke, a real estate and agricultural company owned by the billionaire businessman David Murdock. Murdock continued to expand the island's pineapple production and also developed tourism on the island, building the luxurious Manele Bay Hotel and the exclusive Koele Lodge.

In 2012, Murdock sold the island to Larry Ellison, the co-founder of Oracle Corporation and one of the world's wealthiest individuals. Ellison has since invested heavily in the island, renovating the hotels and developing new tourism attractions, including a world-class golf course and a luxury yacht marina.

Lanai is a unique blend of its rich Polynesian heritage and its more recent history as a pineapple and tourism destination. Despite its small size, the island offers visitors a wide range of activities, from hiking and swimming in pristine natural areas to fine dining and shopping in luxury boutiques.

NiiHau

Niihau is one of the eight main islands in the Hawaiian archipelago and is located southwest of Kauai, its nearest neighbor. The island, known as the "Forbidden Island," is privately owned and has a rich and unique history. Niihau was formed by a shield volcano and is the smallest inhabited island in Hawaii, with an area of just over 69 square miles. The island was once home to a thriving population of Native Hawaiians, who lived in small, isolated communities and subsisted mainly on fishing and farming.

In 1778, British explorer Captain James Cook became the first European to set foot on Niihau. In the years that followed, the island became a popular stopover for whaling ships and was frequently visited by traders and missionaries. In 1864, King Kamehameha V sold Niihau to Elizabeth Sinclair, a wealthy Scottish woman, for $10,000 in gold. Sinclair and her descendants have owned the island ever since, and it has remained largely untouched by modern development.

During World War II, Niihau played a unique role in the Pacific Theater. In December 1941, after the attack on Pearl Harbor, a Japanese pilot crash-landed on the island and was taken in by two Hawaiian residents of Japanese descent. The pilot, named Shigenori Nishikaichi, was eventually killed in a confrontation with local authorities, making Niihau the only place on US soil to be invaded and occupied by enemy forces during the war.

Niihau is home to around 200 residents, most of whom are Native Hawaiians and descendants of the island's original inhabitants. The island remains largely isolated from the outside world, and access is.

restricted to those with permission from the island's owners.

Despite its small size and relative obscurity, Niihau holds a special place in Hawaiian history and remains an important cultural and ecological treasure. The island's unique ecology, which includes endangered species such as the Niihau O'o bird and the Hawaiian monk seal, has been carefully preserved through a variety of conservation efforts, and the island's traditional Hawaiian culture and way of life continue to thrive.

Kahoolawe

Kahoolawe is a small and uninhabited island located in the Hawaiian archipelago. It is the smallest of the eight main Hawaiian Islands and has a long and fascinating history that stretches back thousands of years.

The first inhabitants of Kahoolawe were likely Polynesians who arrived in Hawaii around 500 AD. These early settlers were skilled navigators and seafarers who relied on the ocean for food, transportation, and trade. They likely used Kahoolawe as a stopover point on their voyages between other islands in the archipelago.

Over the centuries, Kahoolawe played an important role in Hawaiian culture and mythology. According to legend, the island was the home of the god Kanaloa, one of the four major deities in the

Hawaiian pantheon. The island was also known for its abundant resources, including fish, shellfish, and native plants.

In the 18th and 19th centuries, Kahoolawe became a strategic location for whaling and maritime trade. American and European ships would stop at the island to take on supplies of fresh water and provisions. However, the arrival of these outsiders also brought new diseases to the islands, which had a devastating impact on the local population.

During the 20th century, Kahoolawe became the site of extensive military training exercises. During World War II, the island was used as a target for naval artillery and bombing practice. This continued into the Cold War era, when the US military used Kahoolawe as a testing ground for new weapons and technologies.

In the 1970s, however, there was growing concern about the impact of military activity on the island's ecosystem and cultural heritage. Hawaiian activists began to push for the return of Kahoolawe to the local community, and in 1993, the island was officially transferred to the state of Hawaii. Since then, efforts have been made to restore the island's ecosystem and cultural sites, and to honor its importance in Hawaiian history and mythology.

MODERN HAWAIIAN HISTORY

The modern history of Hawaii following World War II is marked by significant changes that shaped the state into what it is today. After the war, Hawaii experienced an economic boom, underwent a significant demographic shift, and became the 50th state of the United States. These developments brought both benefits and challenges to the people of Hawaii.

One of the most significant changes in Hawaii's modern history was the economic transformation that occurred after World War II. The war had brought a surge in military spending and tourism, which fueled the growth of the Hawaiian economy. As the war ended, Hawaii became a popular destination for tourists, and the government invested in infrastructure development to support this industry. The construction of airports, hotels, and roads was a major priority, and it helped to create jobs and drive economic growth.

The rise of tourism in Hawaii also led to a shift in the state's demographics. Many people from the mainland United States began to move to Hawaii to work in the tourism industry, which created a more diverse population. This influx of people from different backgrounds and cultures had a profound impact on Hawaii's social and political landscape.

One of the significant challenges that emerged during this time was the issue of Hawaiian sovereignty. For centuries, Hawaii had been an independent kingdom ruled by native Hawaiians. However, in 1893, the United States overthrew the Hawaiian monarchy and annexed the islands as a territory. After World War II, as Hawaii began to move towards statehood, there was a growing movement for Hawaiian sovereignty.

In 1959, Hawaii became the 50th state of the United States, which brought both benefits and challenges. Statehood brought federal funding for education, infrastructure, and social programs, which helped to improve the lives of many Hawaiians. However, statehood also meant that the federal government had more control over Hawaii's resources, and some Hawaiians felt that their cultural heritage was being threatened by the dominant American culture.

In the years following statehood, Hawaii continued to experience significant economic growth, thanks in large part to the tourism industry. However, there were also growing concerns about the impact of tourism on Hawaii's environment and culture. Many Hawaiians felt that the influx of tourists was eroding their traditional way of life, and there were calls for greater regulation of the industry.

Another significant development in Hawaii's modern history was the rise of the Hawaiian Renaissance in the 1970s. This cultural movement was a response to the growing concerns about the erosion of Hawaiian culture and traditions. It was led by a group of Hawaiian artists, activists, and scholars who sought to revive and celebrate traditional Hawaiian culture. The Hawaiian Renaissance had a significant impact on the state's culture and identity and helped to raise awareness of the importance of preserving Hawaii's unique heritage.

In the years since the Hawaiian Renaissance, Hawaii has continued to evolve and change. The state has become a hub for technology and innovation, and there has been growing interest in sustainable tourism and environmental conservation. Hawaii's history post-World War II has been shaped by a complex interplay of economic, social, and cultural factors, and the state continues to navigate these issues as it moves towards the future.

Historical Hawaiians

King Kamehameha I

King Kamehameha, or Kamehameha the Great, was a legendary Hawaiian leader who founded the Kingdom of Hawaii in 1810. He is known for his military conquests, unification of the Hawaiian Islands, and establishment of a legal system that helped to shape the political and cultural landscape of Hawaii. Born in the late 1700s on the island of Hawaii, Kamehameha was trained in the art of warfare and quickly rose to prominence as a warrior and leader. In the late 1700s and early 1800s, he waged a series of battles and conquests against neighboring chiefs, eventually establishing himself as the supreme ruler of the Hawaiian Islands.

One of his most notable achievements was his unification of the islands under a single ruler. This was a remarkable accomplishment, given the diverse cultures and traditions of the various island communities. Kamehameha's ability to bring these communities together under a common vision of unity and prosperity helped to lay the foundation for the Kingdom of Hawaii.

Kamehameha also established a legal system that was based on traditional Hawaiian customs and beliefs. This system was known as the Kapu system, and it helped to regulate social order and maintain harmony among the people of Hawaii. Under Kamehameha's rule, the Kapu system was codified and enforced throughout the kingdom.

Kamehameha is remembered as one of the most influential figures in Hawaiian history. His legacy as a warrior, leader, and unifier is celebrated throughout the islands, and his contributions to Hawaiian culture and society continue to be recognized and honored.

QUEEN LiLiUOKALANi

Queen Liliuokalani was the last monarch of the Kingdom of Hawaii and a pivotal figure in Hawaiian history. Born in 1838, she ascended to the throne in 1891 following the death of her brother, King Kalakaua. Liliuokalani was a strong and independent leader who sought to protect Hawaiian sovereignty and resist American influence in Hawaii.

One of Liliuokalani's most significant accomplishments was her advocacy for a new constitution that would restore power to the monarchy and limit the influence of foreign interests in Hawaii. This new constitution, known as the Bayonet Constitution, had been forced upon her brother by a group of American businessmen in 1887. Liliuokalani was determined to repeal this constitution and restore power to the monarchy. However, her efforts were met with resistance from the same group of businessmen, who were backed by the United States government.

In 1893, a group of American businessmen and

American troops overthrew the Hawaiian monarchy in a coup d'etat. Liliuokalani was imprisoned in her palace and forced to abdicate the throne. Despite this, she continued to advocate for Hawaiian sovereignty and cultural preservation until her death in 1917.

Liliuokalani was also a prolific composer and musician, and she wrote many songs that are still beloved today. One of her most famous compositions is "Aloha Oe," which is often considered Hawaii's unofficial anthem. Queen Liliuokalani is remembered as a symbol of Hawaiian resistance and sovereignty. Her legacy as a strong and independent leader who fought to protect Hawaiian culture and traditions continues to inspire Hawaiians and others around the world.

DUKE KaHaNamoku

Duke Kahanamoku was a legendary Hawaiian surfer, Olympic swimmer, and cultural ambassador who is widely regarded as the father of modern surfing. Born in Honolulu, Hawaii in 1890, Kahanamoku grew up surfing the waves off the coast of Waikiki and quickly developed a reputation as one of the most skilled surfers in the world. In addition to his surfing prowess, Kahanamoku was also an accomplished swimmer, winning multiple Olympic medals for the United States in the early 1900s. His success in swimming helped to bring attention to Hawaii and its culture, and he became a popular ambassador for the state wherever he traveled.

Kahanamoku's most significant contribution to the world, however, was his role in popularizing the sport of surfing. He introduced surfing to the mainland United States and other parts of the world, helping to spark a global fascination with the sport. Kahanamoku's surfing exhibitions and demonstrations helped to raise awareness of Hawaiian culture and values, and he was known for promoting the spirit of aloha, or love and kindness, wherever he went.

Kahanamoku is remembered as a cultural icon and a symbol of Hawaiian pride and identity. His legacy as a surfer, swimmer, and ambassador for Hawaiian culture continues to inspire people around the world, and his influence on modern surfing and watersports is still felt today.

MARY KAWENA PUKUI

Mary Kawena Pukui was a prominent Hawaiian scholar, ethnographer, and linguist who dedicated her life to preserving and promoting Hawaiian culture, language, and traditions. Born in 1895 on the island of Oahu, Pukui grew up speaking Hawaiian and was raised in a family that placed a strong emphasis on cultural traditions.

Pukui's work focused on documenting and studying the Hawaiian language, as well as preserving traditional Hawaiian customs and beliefs. She worked tirelessly to collect and record stories, songs, and other cultural artifacts, which helped to preserve and promote Hawaiian culture for future generations.

One of Pukui's most significant contributions to Hawaiian scholarship was her collaboration with Samuel H. Elbert on the Hawaiian-English Dictionary, which was first published in 1957. The dictionary is widely regarded as the definitive source on the Hawaiian language, and it has been instrumental in helping to preserve and promote the language for future generations.

In addition to her work as a scholar and linguist, Pukui was also an advocate for cultural preservation and revitalization. She worked to promote Hawaiian cultural practices and traditions, including hula, which had been suppressed for many years under colonial rule.

Pukui's contributions to Hawaiian culture and scholarship have been widely recognized and celebrated. She received numerous awards and honors throughout her life, including the Order of the British Empire, and her work continues to be studied and appreciated by scholars and cultural practitioners today.

Historical Hawaiian Cities

Hawaii: Hilo

Hilo is a city located on the eastern coast of the island of Hawaii. It is the largest city on the island after the capital, Honolulu, and has a rich history that is closely tied to the natural beauty and resources of the surrounding area.

The history of Hilo dates back to ancient times, when the area was first settled by Polynesian voyagers who arrived on the island over a thousand years ago. These early settlers were skilled farmers, fishermen, and navigators, and they established a thriving community in the fertile lands surrounding Hilo Bay. In the 19th century, Hilo became an important center of trade and commerce for the island, with a thriving whaling industry and a bustling port. Sugar plantations were also established in the area, and they played a significant role in the local economy for many years.

During World War II, Hilo played an important role in the war effort, serving as a hub for military operations in the Pacific. The city was also hit hard by the devastating tsunami that struck the island in 1946, which caused widespread destruction and loss of life.

In recent years, Hilo has become a popular tourist destination, thanks in large part to its natural beauty and the many attractions in the surrounding area. Visitors can explore the lush rainforests and waterfalls of nearby Wailuku River State Park, as well as the beautiful beaches and coral reefs that line the coast.

Hilo is a thriving city that celebrates its rich history and cultural heritage. From its ancient Polynesian roots to its role in modern Hawaiian society, Hilo has a unique and fascinating history that is closely tied to the land and the people who call it home.

Kailua-Kona

Kailua-Kona is a town on the western coast of the Big Island of Hawaii. Its history dates back to ancient times when it was a bustling center of trade and commerce for the Hawaiian people. In the modern era, Kailua-Kona has become a popular tourist destination known for its beautiful beaches, rich history, and cultural significance. The town was originally known as Kailua, which means "two seas" in Hawaiian, and was an important center of trade and commerce for the Hawaiian people. In the 1800s, Kailua became a hub for the whaling industry, and the town's economy grew rapidly as a result.

During the 1900s, Kailua-Kona became a popular destination for tourists, drawn by the town's natural beauty, rich history, and cultural significance. Today, Kailua-Kona is known for its beautiful beaches, crystal-clear waters, and rich cultural heritage. Visitors can explore the town's historic landmarks, including Hulihe'e Palace, which was once a royal summer home and is now a museum dedicated to Hawaiian history and culture.

One of the most significant events in Kailua-Kona's history was the arrival of Captain James Cook in 1779. Cook was the first European to visit Hawaii, and his arrival had a profound impact on the Hawaiian people and their culture. Cook was killed by Hawaiian warriors during his visit, and his death marked the beginning of a tumultuous period in Hawaiian history as the islands became increasingly subject to foreign influence and colonialism.

Despite the challenges of colonialism and globalization, Kailua-Kona has remained a vibrant and culturally significant place. Its rich history and natural beauty continue to draw visitors from around the world, and the town remains an important center of Hawaiian culture and identity.

Waimea

Waimea is a small town located on the west side of the island of Hawaii, also known as the Big Island. The town has a rich history that dates back to ancient Hawaiian times, and it has played an important role in the cultural and economic development of the island.

The name Waimea means "reddish water" in Hawaiian, and it is believed to have been given to the town because of the reddish hue of the local streams and rivers. The area around Waimea was first settled by ancient Hawaiian communities, who used the fertile land for farming and fishing.

In the late 18th century, the town of Waimea became an important center of commerce and trade for the island. Western traders and merchants began to establish businesses in the town, and it quickly became a hub for the export of sandalwood, which was highly valued in Asia. During the 19th century, Waimea became an important center of missionary activity. Christian missionaries established schools and churches in the town, and they played a significant role in shaping the cultural and social landscape of the community.

Waimea is known for its picturesque setting and rich cultural heritage. The town is surrounded by rolling hills and green valleys, and it is home to several historic sites and landmarks, including the Hawaiian Homestead Community Center and the Parker Ranch, which is one of the largest ranches in the United States.

The history of Waimea is a testament to the enduring legacy of Hawaiian culture and the resilience of its people. Despite the challenges of colonialism and modernization, the town has remained a vibrant and thriving community that continues to celebrate and preserve its unique heritage.

Historical Hawaiian Cities

Maui: Kahului

Kahului is a town located on the island of Maui in the state of Hawaii. The town has a rich history that is closely tied to the development of the sugarcane industry in Hawaii. In the late 1800s, sugarcane was rapidly becoming one of Hawaii's most important industries. Large plantations were established throughout the islands, and thousands of workers were brought in from other countries to work on the plantations. Kahului was one of the key towns that developed around the sugarcane industry on Maui.

In the early 20th century, Kahului became a hub for transportation and commerce. The construction of a deepwater harbor in the town in 1901 helped to facilitate the shipping of sugarcane and other goods to and from Maui. The town also became an important transportation hub, with a major airport and several major highways passing through the area. During World War II, Kahului played a significant role in the war effort. The town's airport was used as a major military airbase, and thousands of troops passed through the town on their way to other parts of the Pacific theater.

After the war, Kahului continued to grow and develop as a center of commerce and transportation. The sugarcane industry remained an important part of the town's economy until the 1990s, when declining profits and increased competition led many of the plantations to close down. Today, Kahului is a bustling town with a diverse economy that includes tourism, agriculture, and technology. The town's rich history and cultural heritage continue to be celebrated and preserved by its residents and visitors alike.

Lahaina

Lahaina is a historic town located on the west coast of the island of Maui in Hawaii. It was once the capital of the Kingdom of Hawaii and served as an important center for the whaling industry in the 19th century. Lahaina was first settled in the early 1800s by whalers, missionaries, and traders. These early settlers were attracted to the area because of its strategic location, sheltered harbor, and abundant natural resources. Over time, Lahaina grew into a bustling town, with a thriving economy and a rich cultural and social scene.

One of the most significant events in Lahaina's history was the establishment of the first Christian church in Hawaii in 1823. The Waine'e Church, played a role in the spread of Christianity throughout the islands and is still in use today. In the mid-19th century, Lahaina became a major center for the whaling industry. Whaling ships from all over the world would anchor in Lahaina's harbor, and the town's economy boomed as a result.

Today, Lahaina is a popular tourist destination, known for its historic sites, beautiful beaches, and vibrant cultural scene. Many of the town's historic buildings and landmarks have been preserved, including the Waine'e Church and the Baldwin Home Museum, which was once the residence of a prominent missionary family.

Wailea

Wailea is a resort area located on the southwestern coast of Maui, Hawaii. Its history is rooted in Hawaiian tradition and culture, and it has since become a popular destination for visitors seeking a luxurious and relaxing vacation experience. The area of Wailea was originally inhabited by native Hawaiians, who utilized the land for fishing, farming, and other cultural practices. In the early 1800s, the area was purchased by the ruling chiefs of Maui, and it remained under their control until the overthrow of the Hawaiian monarchy in 1893.

Following the overthrow of the monarchy, the land was sold to foreign investors, and much of it was converted into sugarcane plantations. The area remained relatively undeveloped until the mid-20th century when tourism began to emerge as a major industry in Hawaii. In the 1970s, a development plan was created for Wailea, which called for the creation of a luxury resort area that would cater to high-end travelers. The plan was implemented, and over the following decades, Wailea grew into one of the most popular resort destinations in Hawaii.

Today, Wailea is known for its beautiful beaches, world-class golf courses, and luxurious resorts. It is a popular destination for visitors seeking a relaxing and upscale vacation experience, and it continues to be an important economic driver for Maui and the state of Hawaii. Despite its transformation into a resort destination, Wailea remains rooted in Hawaiian culture and traditions. The area is home to numerous cultural sites, including ancient Hawaiian fishponds and sacred sites, which serve as a reminder of its rich history and cultural heritage.

Historical Hawaiian Cities

Oahu: Honolulu

Honolulu, the capital and largest city of Hawaii, has a rich and varied history that stretches back over a thousand years. The city is situated on the southern coast of the island of Oahu and is home to over 350,000 people. The earliest known settlement in the Honolulu area dates back to around 1100 AD, when Polynesian voyagers first arrived in the Hawaiian Islands. For centuries, the area was home to fishing villages and agricultural communities, which were organized into small chiefdoms.

In the late 1700s, European explorers, including Captain James Cook, arrived in Hawaii and began to establish trade relationships with the islanders. This led to significant changes in Hawaiian society, including the introduction of Western goods and technologies. In 1804, Honolulu was established as a port town and became an important center of trade and commerce. The city continued to grow and develop throughout the 19th century, as the Hawaiian Kingdom came into contact with other colonial powers, including the United States.

In 1893, American businessmen overthrew the Hawaiian monarchy and established a provisional government in Honolulu. The city became the capital of the newly formed Territory of Hawaii in 1900 and played an important role in the growth and development of the islands.

During World War II, Honolulu became a key military hub for the United States, with the construction of the Pearl Harbor Naval Base and other military installations. The city was also the site of the Japanese attack on Pearl Harbor in 1941, which propelled the United States into the war. In the post-war years, Honolulu experienced significant growth and development, particularly in the tourism industry. The city is now a major destination for visitors from around the world, who come to enjoy its beaches, cultural attractions, and natural beauty.

Waikiki

Waikiki is a famous beachfront neighborhood in Honolulu, Hawaii that is known for its beautiful beaches, high-rise hotels, and vibrant nightlife. The area has a rich history that dates back to ancient Hawaiian times, when it was considered a sacred area for Hawaiian royalty.

In the 1800s, Waikiki began to attract visitors from around the world, who were drawn to the area's pristine beaches and warm climate. Many wealthy individuals built homes in the area, and it soon became a popular vacation destination for the elite.

The opening of the Moana Hotel in 1901 helped to cement Waikiki's reputation as a world-class resort destination. The hotel was a luxurious property that attracted wealthy travelers from around the world, and it helped to spur the development of other high-end hotels in the area.

During World War II, Waikiki played an important role as a military hub for the United States. The area was home to several military bases, and it served as a staging ground for military operations in the Pacific theater. In the post-war era, Waikiki underwent significant development as the tourism industry continued to grow. The area became known for its high-rise hotels, luxury shopping, and lively entertainment scene. Today, Waikiki is one of the most popular tourist destinations in the world, attracting millions of visitors each year.

Kailua

Kailua is a coastal town on the windward side of the island of Oahu in Hawaii. The history of Kailua dates back to ancient times, when it was a thriving fishing village and agricultural center. Over the centuries, Kailua has undergone significant changes, from being a Hawaiian royal retreat to a popular tourist destination. In ancient times, Kailua was a center of Hawaiian culture and trade. The area was known for its rich fisheries, which provided a source of food for the local people. Kailua was also an important center for agriculture, with taro, sweet potato, and other crops grown in the fertile soil of the surrounding hills.

During the 17th and 18th centuries, Kailua became an important center of Hawaiian royalty. The area was home to several Hawaiian monarchs, including King Kamehameha I, who had a residence in Kailua. The area became a hub of political and cultural activity, with hula and other traditional Hawaiian arts flourishing. In the 20th century, Kailua began to experience significant growth and development. The construction of a bridge over Kaelepulu Stream in the 1940s made the area more accessible, and it began to attract tourists looking for a peaceful getaway. In the 1960s and 70s, Kailua experienced a housing boom, with new subdivisions and homes being built to accommodate a growing population.

Today, Kailua is a popular tourist destination, known for its beautiful beaches, scenic hikes, and laid-back lifestyle. The area has retained much of its natural beauty and small-town charm, and it continues to attract visitors from around the world who are drawn to its unique mix of history, culture, and natural beauty.

Historical Hawaiian Cities

Kauai: Lihue

Lihue is a town located on the eastern side of the island of Kauai in Hawaii. The town is the commercial and governmental center of Kauai and has a rich history that reflects the island's unique culture and heritage. Lihue was originally settled by Native Hawaiians who lived in the area for hundreds of years before the arrival of Europeans. The town was an important center for agriculture, and Native Hawaiians grew taro, sweet potatoes, and other crops in the fertile soil of the surrounding area.

In the late 1700s, Lihue and the rest of Kauai came under the rule of King Kamehameha I, who unified the Hawaiian Islands under his rule. During the 1800s, Lihue continued to thrive as an agricultural center, and the town became an important hub for the production of sugar cane and other crops. In the early 1900s, Lihue began to experience significant growth and development. The construction of Lihue Plantation Company's sugar mill and the opening of the Kauai Railway helped to spur economic growth and bring new people and ideas to the town. During World War II, Lihue played an important role in the Pacific theater. The town's airport was used as a military base, and the surrounding area was home to numerous military installations.

Today, Lihue is a thriving community that

blends its rich history with modern amenities and attractions. Visitors to the town can explore historic sites like Kilohana Plantation, which dates back to the 1930s, or the Kauai Museum, which showcases the island's rich cultural heritage. Lihue is also a hub for shopping, dining, and entertainment, and the town continues to be an important center for agriculture and tourism on Kauai.

HANALEI

Hanalei is a small town located on the north shore of the Hawaiian island of Kauai. The town is known for its picturesque setting, beautiful beaches, and rich cultural history. The name Hanalei comes from the Hawaiian words "hana" and "lei," which mean "work" and "wreath," respectively. The town is named after a legend in which a goddess named Hina worked to create a lei of stars, which she then threw into the sky.

In the early 19th century, Hanalei became an important center for the sugar industry, which brought a wave of immigrants to the area. Many of these immigrants were from China, Japan, and the Philippines, and their cultural influences can still be seen in the town today. During the mid-20th century, Hanalei became a popular destination for surfers and hippies, who were drawn to the town's laid-back vibe and beautiful scenery. This influx of visitors helped to establish Hanalei as a cultural and artistic center, and many notable musicians, artists, and writers have spent time in the town over the years.

Today, Hanalei is a thriving community that celebrates its cultural heritage while embracing modern amenities and conveniences. Visitors can explore the town's historic sites, including the Waioli Mission House, which was built in 1837 and is now a museum. The town is also home to several art galleries, boutiques, and restaurants, which offer a taste of local cuisine and culture. Despite its popularity with tourists, Hanalei has managed to maintain its small-town charm and sense of community. The town remains a testament to the rich cultural history and natural beauty of the Hawaiian islands.

POIPU

Poipu is a coastal town located on the southern shore of the island of Kauai, Hawaii. The history of Poipu dates back to ancient times, when it was a fishing village for the Hawaiian people. The name "Poipu" means "crashing waves" in the Hawaiian language, which reflects the area's rugged coastline and strong ocean currents.

In the 19th century, Poipu became a popular destination for plantation owners, who built homes and resorts in the area. The first hotel in Poipu, the Poipu Hotel, was built in 1846 and became a popular destination for wealthy travelers from the mainland United States. The hotel was destroyed in a fire in 1919, but its legacy lived on as the area continued to attract tourists and investors.

In the mid-20th century, Poipu experienced a

period of rapid development as the tourism industry boomed. New hotels, restaurants, and shops were built in the area, and Poipu became a popular destination for visitors from around the world. However, this growth also had a significant impact on the environment and local culture, and there were growing concerns about the impact of tourism on the area.

Today, Poipu is a popular destination for tourists who come to enjoy the area's beaches, snorkeling, and other outdoor activities. The town has worked to balance tourism with environmental conservation and cultural preservation, and there are numerous organizations and initiatives focused on preserving the area's unique heritage and natural resources. Despite the changes that have occurred over the years, Poipu remains a special place with a rich history and vibrant culture. Visitors to the area can experience the beauty of the natural environment, learn about the area's history and culture, and connect with the local community in meaningful ways.

PEARL HARBOR & IOLANI PALACE
PEARL HARBOR

On December 7, 1941, the Imperial Japanese Navy launched a surprise attack on the United States naval base at Pearl Harbor, located on the island of Oahu in Hawaii. The attack led to the entry of the United States into World War II and marked a turning point in the conflict. In the late 19th century, the United States annexed Hawaii and established a naval base at Pearl Harbor, which is a natural deep-water harbor that offered strategic advantages. The base was expanded over the years, and by the 1930s, it was one of the largest naval bases in the world. The base was home to the Pacific Fleet, which included battleships, cruisers, and aircraft carriers.

At the time, tensions between Japan and the United States were high. Japan had embarked on a campaign of imperial expansion in the Pacific and Asia, and the United States had opposed these actions. The two countries had been negotiating for years over various issues, including Japan's desire for natural resources and the United States' desire to protect China. The negotiations between the two countries came to a head in November 1941, when the United States presented Japan with an ultimatum, demanding that Japan withdraw its forces from China and Southeast Asia. Japan viewed the demand as a threat to its national security and decided to take pre-emptive action.

On the morning of December 7, 1941, a fleet

of Japanese planes launched a surprise attack on Pearl Harbor. The attack began at 7:55 a.m. local time and lasted for two hours. The Japanese planes targeted the battleships, aircraft, and fuel storage facilities at the base. The attack resulted in the deaths of 2,403 Americans, including civilians and military personnel, and the destruction of numerous ships and aircraft. The attack was a tactical success for Japan, but it was also a strategic mistake. The attack provoked the United States to declare war on Japan and led to the entry of the United States into World War II. It also united the American people and strengthened their resolve to defeat Japan and the other Axis powers.

In the days following the attack, the United States mobilized its military and industrial resources to fight the war. The country rallied around the slogan "Remember Pearl Harbor" and vowed to avenge the attack. The United States declared war on Japan the following day, and Germany and Italy declared war on the United States a few days later, bringing the United States fully into World War II. In the months and years that followed, the United States and its allies fought a long and brutal war against Japan and the other Axis powers. The war ultimately ended in victory for the United States and its allies, with Japan surrendering in August 1945.

Today, Pearl Harbor is a national historic site and a place of remembrance for the Americans who lost their lives in the attack. The site includes the

USS Arizona Memorial, which marks the final resting place of many of the sailors and Marines who died on the battleship during the attack. The attack on Pearl Harbor remains a significant event in American history, reminding us of the sacrifices made by the men and women who fought in World War II and the importance of remaining vigilant in the face of threats to our national security.

IOLANI PALACE

Iolani Palace is a significant landmark in the history of Hawaii, situated in the downtown area of Honolulu. The palace is a striking symbol of Hawaiian sovereignty and monarchy, and it is the only royal palace in the United States. The palace was constructed in 1882, and it served as the residence for the Hawaiian monarchy until the overthrow of the monarchy in 1893.

The palace was designed by a Scottish architect named Thomas J. Baker, who was influenced by the European neoclassical style. The building's distinctive features include its ornate façade, grand staircase, and large lanai or balcony. It was constructed using materials from around the world, including Oregon pine, Vermont granite, and Italian marble.

The construction of the palace was commissioned by King Kalakaua, who was determined to establish a grand royal residence that would befit the prestige of Hawaii's monarchy. The palace was named "Iolani" in honor of his predecessor, King Kamehameha V, who had passed away in 1872. The palace was designed to serve not only as a royal residence but also as a center of political and social life for the Hawaiian monarchy. It featured a grand hall for royal receptions and balls, as well as private apartments for the king and queen, guest rooms, and offices for government officials.

After the death of King Kalakaua in 1891, his sister, Queen Liliuokalani, succeeded him to the throne. However, her reign was short-lived, as a group of American businessmen, aided by the U.S. Marines, overthrew the Hawaiian monarchy in 1893. The queen was imprisoned in the palace for several months before being placed under house arrest in a nearby residence.

Following the overthrow of the monarchy, Iolani Palace was used as a government building, serving as the executive building for the Republic of Hawaii, the Territory of Hawaii, and finally the State of Hawaii. Over the years, the palace underwent various renovations and changes, including the addition of electricity, plumbing, and telephones. Despite its significance as a symbol of Hawaiian sovereignty and monarchy, the palace fell into disrepair in the early 20th century. However, in the 1960s, a movement to restore the palace gained momentum, and extensive restoration work was carried out in the 1970s and 1980s.

Today, Iolani Palace stands as a testament to Hawaii's rich cultural heritage and the legacy of its monarchy. It is a popular tourist attraction, with thousands of visitors each year coming to explore the palace's grand rooms, historic artifacts, and stunning architecture. In 1978, Iolani Palace was designated a National Historic Landmark, and it was added to the National Register of Historic Places in 1972.

Iolani Palace is a crucial landmark in Hawaiian history, serving as a testament to the legacy of Hawaii's monarchy and its struggle for sovereignty. Despite the upheavals and changes that have taken place over the years, the palace remains a symbol of the pride and resilience of the Hawaiian people, and it stands as a reminder of the rich cultural heritage that has shaped the history of this beautiful island nation.

PUUHONUA O HONAUNAU & KALAUPAPA NATIONAL HISTORICAL PARKS

PUUHONUA O HONAUNAU NATIONAL PARK

Puuhonua o Honaunau National Historical Park is a sacred and historical site located on the Kona Coast of the Big Island of Hawaii. The park is a preserved area that is dedicated to preserving and sharing the history and cultural heritage of Hawaii. The park is one of the most popular tourist destinations on the Big Island and has a rich and fascinating history that dates back to ancient times. The park is situated on a 180-acre piece of land that is surrounded by a stone wall. The wall was built to protect the sacred land and the people who lived there from invaders. The park features several ancient Hawaiian structures, including the Hale o Keawe temple, the Great Wall, and the royal fishponds.

The history of the Puuhonua o Honaunau National Historical Park dates back to the time of the ancient Hawaiians. The area was considered a sacred site and was used as a place of refuge for those who broke the strict laws of the Hawaiian culture. In ancient times, breaking a law in Hawaii was a serious offense that could result in death. Those who broke the law were given a chance to escape punishment by fleeing to a Puuhonua or a sacred place of refuge. The Puuhonua o Honaunau was one of the most important places of refuge in ancient Hawaii. Those who made it to the park were granted immunity from punishment and were able to start a new life. The park was a sacred place where people could seek forgiveness and redemption.

In the late 18th century, the area was used as a royal residence by King Kamehameha I. The king used the park as a place to rest and prepare for battles. The park was also used as a place to store weapons and supplies. In the 19th century, the area became a Christian mission station. The missionaries built a church and a school on the site. The park remained an important religious and cultural site for the Hawaiian people. In 1961, the Puuhonua o Honaunau was declared a National Historical Park by the National Park Service. The park was established to preserve the ancient Hawaiian culture and to share it with visitors from around the world. The park has become a popular tourist destination and attracts thousands of visitors each year.

Today, the Puuhonua o Honaunau National Historical Park is a place where visitors can learn about the ancient Hawaiian culture and the history of Hawaii. Visitors can explore the park's ancient structures, including the Hale o Keawe temple and the Great Wall. The park also features several cultural demonstrations, including traditional Hawaiian music and dance performances. The park is also home to a variety of wildlife, including sea turtles, dolphins, and a wide range of birds. Visitors can hike along the park's scenic trails, swim in the crystal-clear waters of Honaunau Bay, and enjoy the beautiful natural surroundings.

The Puuhonua o Honaunau National Historical Park is a sacred and historical site that has played an important role in the history and culture of Hawaii. The park is a place of refuge and redemption that has been used by the ancient Hawaiians, the Hawaiian kings, and the Christian missionaries. Today, the park is a popular tourist destination that attracts visitors from around the world who come to learn about the rich cultural heritage of Hawaii and to enjoy the natural beauty of the Kona Coast.

Kalaupapa National Park

Kalaupapa National Park is a historic site located on the island of Molokai in Hawaii, USA. The park covers an area of 13,297 acres and is home to a number of natural and cultural resources. The park was established in 1980 to preserve the history of the leprosy settlement that was established on the peninsula in the late 19th century. The park is also home to some of the most stunning views in the world, as the sea cliffs rise dramatically from the ocean to a height of 3,000 feet.

The history of Kalaupapa dates back to the 1860s when the Hawaiian government passed a law that required all people with leprosy to be quarantined. Leprosy, also known as Hansen's disease, was a highly contagious and incurable disease that was feared by the public. At the time, the only treatment for leprosy was to isolate the infected individuals and prevent the spread of the disease.

The government of Hawaii selected the

Kalaupapa Peninsula as the site for the leprosy settlement because of its isolated location. The peninsula is surrounded by sea cliffs on three sides, making it difficult for people to leave or enter the area. The only access to the peninsula was by sea, and the government established a settlement there in 1866.

The first group of people with leprosy arrived at Kalaupapa in 1866, and over the years, thousands of people were sent to live on the peninsula. The settlement was managed by the Hawaiian government until 1884 when it was turned over to the Catholic Church. The Catholic Church managed the settlement until 1969 when the state of Hawaii took over. Life on Kalaupapa was extremely difficult for the people with leprosy. They were isolated from their families and friends and were forced to live in crowded conditions. There were few medical facilities available, and the people with leprosy had to rely on each other for support. Despite the difficult conditions, the people with leprosy managed to create a vibrant community on Kalaupapa.

The settlement on Kalaupapa remained in operation until 1969 when the state of Hawaii lifted the quarantine. Today, Kalaupapa is a National Historical Park, and visitors can take guided tours of the peninsula to learn about the history of the leprosy settlement. The park also contains a museum, a visitor center, and a number of hiking trails. The establishment of Kalaupapa National Park was a significant event in the history of Hawaii. It served as a reminder of the hardships that the people with leprosy faced and the courage and resilience that they demonstrated. The park also serves as a reminder of the need for compassion and understanding when dealing with people who have a disease.

In addition to its cultural significance, Kalaupapa National Park is also home to a number of unique natural features. The sea cliffs that surround the peninsula are among the tallest in the world and offer stunning views of the ocean below. The park is also home to a number of rare and endangered species, including the Hawaiian monk seal and the green sea turtle. Kalaupapa National Park is a unique and important site that offers visitors a glimpse into the history of Hawaii. The park's rich cultural and natural resources make it a popular destination for tourists and a source of pride for the people of Hawaii.

TRADITIONAL HAWAIIAN SPORTS

Hawaii has a rich history of traditional sports that are deeply rooted in the island's culture and history. Many of these sports were practiced by the native Hawaiians for centuries before the arrival of Western explorers and missionaries. Today, these traditional sports continue to be celebrated and enjoyed by both locals and visitors alike.

SURFING

The history of surfing in Hawaii dates back over a thousand years, when Polynesian voyagers first arrived on the islands with their surfing traditions. Ancient Hawaiian culture had a deep connection to the ocean and surfing was a sacred activity that was closely tied to religion and spirituality. Surfing was a way for people to connect with the gods, gain strength and show off their skills.

In the 19th century, Hawaii was discovered by Western explorers and missionaries, who initially frowned upon surfing as a sinful and barbaric activity. However, over time, surfing became popular among the visitors to Hawaii, and by the early 20th century, it had become a tourist attraction. The Duke Kahanamoku, a native Hawaiian, is credited with popularizing surfing as a sport outside of Hawaii. He won gold medals in swimming in the 1912 and 1920 Olympics and used his fame to showcase surfing on the mainland US and Australia. His influence helped to make surfing a mainstream sport and led to the development of surf culture as we know it today.

Hawaii remains a mecca for surfers from around the world, and many of the world's best surfers hail from the islands. The North Shore of Oahu is one of the most famous surf spots in the world, and the Triple Crown of Surfing, a series of three professional surfing events held there every winter, is one of the most prestigious contests in the sport. Today, surfing is an integral part of Hawaiian culture and continues to inspire and thrill surfers of all ages and backgrounds.

CANOEING

Canoeing has a history in Hawaii dating back thousands of years to the Polynesian settlers who first arrived on the islands. The Polynesians were skilled navigators and used outrigger canoes to travel between the islands and fish in the abundant waters surrounding Hawaii. Canoes were not just a means of transportation but also held great cultural significance, often being used in religious ceremonies and cultural festivals. In the late 1700s, European explorers arrived in Hawaii and brought with them new technologies and watercraft. This led to the decline of traditional canoeing in Hawaii, as more modern boats became prevalent. However, in the early 20th century, there was a renewed interest in traditional Hawaiian canoeing, and a movement to revive and preserve the ancient art began.

This led to the formation of the Hawaiian Canoe Racing Association in 1954, which established rules and regulations for canoe racing in Hawaii. The association has since grown to include over 100 member clubs and thousands of participants, and the annual Molokai Hoe race, which takes paddlers across the treacherous Kaiwi Channel between Molokai and Oahu, has become a highly anticipated event.

Today, canoeing is an important part of Hawaiian culture and is practiced by people of all ages and backgrounds. The use of traditional outrigger canoes has also expanded beyond just racing, with many clubs offering cultural and educational programs centered around canoeing. The legacy of canoeing in Hawaii continues to thrive and evolve, with new generations carrying on the traditions of their ancestors.

HULA

The hula is a traditional dance of Hawaii that has been an integral part of the island's culture for centuries. The origins of the hula date back to ancient times when the Polynesians first arrived in Hawaii, and it was used as a form of storytelling and religious ritual. The dance was performed by both men and women and was accompanied by chanting and music played on instruments such as the ukulele, the guitar, and the ipu (a gourd drum). Hula was a way of passing down stories, legends, and history from generation to generation.

During the 19th century, when Hawaii was under the rule of the Hawaiian Kingdom, hula faced a period of suppression. The missionaries who came to the islands regarded the dance as being immoral and tried to ban it. As a result, hula was performed in secret and was passed down only within families. However, in the early 20th century, hula experienced a revival thanks to the efforts of King David Kalakaua, who believed that hula was an important part of Hawaiian culture that needed to be preserved. He organized hula competitions, which helped to revive interest in the dance.

Today, hula is still an essential part of Hawaiian culture and is performed at festivals, weddings, and other important events. There are two main types of hula: the hula kahiko, which is a traditional dance, and the hula auana, which is a modern form of hula that incorporates Western influences.

Makahiki Games

Makahiki Games is a traditional Hawaiian festival that is deeply rooted in the history and culture of the Hawaiian people. It is a time for giving thanks to the gods and celebrating the harvest season, which typically falls between October and February. The Makahiki Games were held every year throughout the islands of Hawaii and were celebrated with feasting, dancing, and athletic competitions. The games were an opportunity for the Hawaiian people to come together and honor their gods, as well as to strengthen their bonds as a community.

The origins of the Makahiki Games can be

traced back to ancient Hawaiian mythology, where the god Lono was said to have traveled to the islands on a long journey. During his travels, he taught the Hawaiians the art of agriculture and introduced them to the Makahiki festival, which became an annual event. The Makahiki Games were an important part of Hawaiian culture and were observed until the late 1800s, when they were banned by the Christian missionaries who arrived in Hawaii. However, in recent years, there has been a revival of interest in the Makahiki Games, and they have once again become an important part of Hawaiian cultural heritage.

Today, the Makahiki Games are celebrated on many of the Hawaiian islands, and they continue to be a time for giving thanks, celebrating the harvest, and strengthening the bonds of community. The games include traditional Hawaiian athletic competitions such as foot races, canoe races, and spear throwing, as well as cultural events such as hula dancing and feasting. The Makahiki Games are a living testament to the enduring cultural heritage of the Hawaiian people.

Hawaiian Boxing

Hawaiian boxing, also known as Lua, is an ancient Hawaiian martial art that was used for self-defense, as well as for warfare. It is believed that the origins of Lua can be traced back to the early Polynesians who migrated to Hawaii from other parts of the Pacific.

Lua was traditionally taught by Hawaiian

warriors known as Kahuna Lua. These warriors were highly skilled in the art of Lua, and their training was rigorous and intense. They would practice fighting techniques, as well as herbal medicine, spiritual practices, and weapon skills. Lua was used in many battles throughout Hawaii's history, including the wars between the Hawaiian islands. It was also used to defend against foreign invaders, such as Captain Cook and his crew, who were met with fierce resistance from Hawaiian warriors trained in Lua.

During the 19th century, the practice of Lua began to decline due to the influence of Western culture and the introduction of firearms. However, efforts have been made to revive the art of Lua, and it is still practiced today by some Hawaiian families and martial artists. In recent years, there has been a growing interest in Lua, and it is now recognized as an important part of Hawaiian culture. Many people are drawn to Lua not only for its practical self-defense applications but also for its rich cultural history and spiritual practices.
origins of Lua can be traced back to the early Polynesians who migrated to Hawaii from other parts of the Pacific.

Lua was traditionally taught by Hawaiian warriors known as Kahuna Lua. These warriors were highly skilled in the art of Lua, and their training was rigorous and intense. They would practice fighting techniques, as well as herbal medicine, spiritual practices, and weapon skills. Lua was used in many battles throughout Hawaii's history, including the wars between the Hawaiian islands. It was also used to defend against foreign invaders, such as Captain Cook and his crew, who were met with fierce resistance from Hawaiian warriors trained in Lua.

During the 19th century, the practice of Lua began to decline due to the influence of Western culture and the introduction of firearms. However, efforts have been made to revive the art of Lua, and it is still practiced today by some Hawaiian families and martial artists. In recent years, there has been a growing interest in Lua, and it is now recognized as an important part of Hawaiian culture. Many people are drawn to Lua not only for its practical self-defense applications but also for its rich cultural history and spiritual practices.

Hawaiian Foods

Historical Hawaiian foods refer to the traditional foods that were eaten by the native Hawaiians prior to the arrival of Europeans. These foods were primarily plant-based and consisted of fruits, vegetables, and roots, as well as fish and other seafood. These are just a few examples of the historical Hawaiian foods that have been passed down through generations of native Hawaiians. Many of these foods are still popular today and are enjoyed by both locals and visitors to the islands.

Poi

Poi is a traditional food of the Hawaiian people, made from the root of the taro plant. The history of poi in Hawaii is intertwined with the culture and identity of the indigenous people of Hawaii, known as the Kanaka Maoli. Poi has been a staple food in Hawaii for centuries and is often referred to as the "staff of life."

The cultivation of taro and the production of poi have been integral to Hawaiian society for over a thousand years. The process of making poi involves pounding cooked taro roots into a smooth paste, which is then mixed with water to achieve the desired consistency. The resulting product is a thick, sticky, and slightly sour substance that can be eaten alone or used as a base for other dishes.

Poi played a significant role in Hawaiian culture, serving as a symbol of unity and social cohesion. It was traditionally eaten with the fingers, and the communal act of sharing a bowl of poi was seen as a way to strengthen the bonds between people. Poi was also used in religious ceremonies and as a medicinal food, believed to have healing properties.

During the 19th century, the arrival of missionaries and Westerners in Hawaii brought significant changes to Hawaiian society, including a decline in the consumption of poi. However, in recent years, there has been a renewed interest in Hawaiian traditions and culture, and poi has experienced a resurgence in popularity. Today, poi is widely available throughout Hawaii, and many Hawaiians continue to view it as an important part of their cultural heritage.

Kalua Pig

Kalua pig is a traditional Hawaiian dish that is made by slow-cooking a whole pig in an underground oven, called an imu, until it becomes tender and succulent. The history of Kalua pig in Hawaii dates back to ancient times, when it was a staple food for the Hawaiian people and was often served during special occasions and ceremonies.

The traditional method of cooking Kalua pig in an imu involves digging a pit in the ground and lining it with rocks. A fire is built on top of the rocks, and the pig is placed in the pit and covered with banana leaves and burlap sacks. The pig is then left to cook for several hours, during which time it absorbs the flavors of the smoke and the rocks, resulting in a delicious and unique taste.

The origins of Kalua pig are rooted in Hawaiian mythology, which tells the story of the god Kamapua'a, who was half-man, half-pig. Legend has it that Kamapua'a taught the Hawaiians how to prepare and cook pork, and that Kalua pig was his favorite dish. Today, Kalua pig remains a popular dish in Hawaii and is served at luaus, weddings, and other special events. While the traditional method of cooking it in an imu is still practiced, modern methods involve using a slow cooker or a roasting pan in an oven. Regardless of the method, the flavor of Kalua pig remains a beloved part of Hawaiian culture and cuisine.

POKE

Poke, which means "to cut into pieces" in Hawaiian, has a long and rich history in Hawaii. The dish is typically made with raw fish, seasoned with salt, seaweed, and other spices, and served as a snack or appetizer.

The origins of poke can be traced back to ancient Hawaiian fishing traditions. Fishermen would often catch fish and immediately cut them into bite-sized pieces, which were then seasoned with salt and eaten raw. This simple yet delicious preparation method eventually became a staple of Hawaiian cuisine. Over time, different regions of Hawaii developed their own variations of poke, each with its own unique flavor and ingredients. For example, in the early 20th century, Japanese immigrants introduced shoyu (soy sauce) and sesame oil to the dish, giving it a richer and more complex flavor profile.

Poke continued to gain popularity throughout the 20th century, with many restaurants and markets in Hawaii specializing in the dish. In recent years, poke has become a global food trend, with poke bowls and sushi burritos popping up on menus all over the world. Despite its global popularity, poke remains deeply rooted in Hawaiian culture and tradition. It continues to be a beloved dish among locals and visitors alike, and is an important part of Hawaii's culinary heritage.

WELCOME TO HAWAII!

KID PLANET BOOKS ARE WRITTEN TO HELP CHILDREN LEARN!

KID PLANET BOOKS

LOGAN STOVER IS A HISTORIAN, EDUCATOR, & THE CREATOR OF KID PLANET CHILDREN'S BOOKS!

"LOGAN HAS A GIFT FOR TEACHING HISTORY TO ALL AGES. HE MAKES LEARNING FUN!"

www.KIDPLANETBOOKS.com

@LEARN.WITH.LOGAN

Made in the USA
Monee, IL
26 March 2025

14658058R00049